FACE
FACE

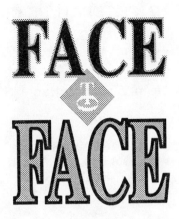

FACE to FACE

Glimpses into the
Inner Life of Moses the Man of God

with which is incorporated

Union with Christ
in Death and Resurrection

By
JESSIE PENN-LEWIS

CHRISTIAN • LITERATURE • CRUSADE
Fort Washington, Pennsylvania 19034

CHRISTIAN LITERATURE CRUSADE

U.S.A.
Box 1449, Fort Washington, PA 19034

BRITAIN
51 The Dean, Alresford, Hants. SO24 9BJ

Originally published by
THE OVERCOMER LITERATURE TRUST
England

ISBN 0-87508-942-9

Cover photo: Superstock/Kogi Kitagawa

Scripture Quotations from:
The King James Version unless otherwise
   indicated.
The American Standard Version (*ASV*),
   1901, Thomas Nelson & Sons, New
   York.
The Epistles of Paul (a translation and
   notes) by W. J. Conybeare (died 1857).

PRINTED IN THE UNITED STATES OF AMERICA

CONTENTS

PREFACE

"FACE TO FACE" should be the hallmark of every "Quiet Hour" spent alone with God, but it is to be feared that despite all the knowledge of today, not all God's children know their God so as to have that direct intercourse with Him which is described in the suggestive words of our title. There is a fellowship with God which is "sight" to the "eyes of the heart," even though in comparison with the full vision that is yet to come "we see through a glass darkly."

There is a face-to-face fellowship with God where we "inquire of the Lord" as David did, and get our answer; where we have such communion with Him that He is able to reveal His mind to us, and where we intelligently know and enter into the purposes of our God.

With regard to the "Quiet Hour" for which the message of this book is especially written, let us turn to the history of Moses in order to gather instruction in the "vision of God," and by glimpses into Moses' inner life see how he was led from the court of

Egypt to the "Presence chamber" of the King of kings. *"There arose not a prophet since in Israel like unto Moses, whom the LORD knew face to face,"* runs the sacred record (Deuteronomy 34:10). And yet Moses once lived in a worldly home—even in a heathen court—and had to decide to follow Christ, just like other men. Step by step he learned to know the Lord, and to follow Him fully, until he was granted a friendship with the Eternal God such as few have ever known.

Do we say, "For Moses, face-to-face knowledge of God may have been possible, but for *me*, in *my* circumstances and in the very different conditions of the present age, it cannot be"?

Surely Moses could also have said that *his* circumstances were against him! He could have said: "Abraham, in his peaceful tent life, away from the heathen palace of Pharaoh, might have face-to-face communion with Jehovah—but for *me* in Egypt, with *my* surroundings, it is impossible!"

We are reminded in Hebrews 3:5 that Moses was a servant in the house of God over which Christ is the Son and Heir. But we have been brought into union with the Son and given the place of children, and "if children, then heirs; heirs of God, and joint-heirs with Christ" (Romans 8:17).

"Face-to-face" fellowship with God is our birthright as children of God, and if we are but willing to follow on to know the Lord we shall be led by the Spirit from faith to faith, and glory to glory, until we are in reality "no longer . . . servants . . . but friends."

"Face-to-face" fellowship means that anywhere, at any moment, we may have spiritual communion with Him who is invisible, and hear His voice in our hearts speaking to us, across the blood-sprinkled mercy-seat.

As we wait before our God let us cry, "Thy face, Lord, will I seek"; so will He cause His face to shine upon us, and we shall walk habitually in the light of His countenance, see His glory, and speak of Him.

"Show me Thy face—one transient gleam of loveliness Divine,
And I shall never think or dream of other love save Thine:
All lesser light will darken quite, all lower glories wane,
The beautiful of earth will scarce seem beautiful again."

CHAPTER 1

LIFE OUT OF DEATH

"She called his name Moses ['drawn out,' margin]; and she said, Because I drew him out of the water" (Exodus 2:10).

THE birth of Moses and the circumstances attending it picture God's way of salvation for every soul translated out of the power of darkness into the kingdom of God's dear Son.

"Pharaoh charged all his people, saying, Every son that is born ye shall cast into the river" (Exodus 1:22). The sentence of death was passed upon Moses before he was born, but, by faith, the parents were able to hide him for three whole months. When this was no longer possible, the mother placed her helpless babe in an ark of bulrushes, and, committing him to the keeping of the God she trusted in, laid him in the flags by the river's brink. Here the daughter of Pharaoh found him, and he was saved to be brought up as a king's son.

As we read the story of the way Jochebed dealt with her babe we cannot fail to see how God works all things after the counsel of His own will. It was He who guided the mother to the thought of the ark and moved her to commit her treasure to the river, rewarding her faith by giving back, as from death, her lovely babe to nurse for Him. It was as though God said to her through the lips of Pharaoh's daughter, "Take this child away, and nurse it for *Me*, and I will give thee thy wages" (Exodus 2:9).

What a reminder this is of Abraham who with his own hands laid his son upon the altar, "accounting that God was able to raise him up, even from the dead; from whence also he received him in a figure." Thus did Jochebed with her own hands surrender her babe to the waters, reasoning that God was able to save him from death, which He actually did.

Is this not the wondrous story of redemption, given us in one of God's many picture lessons? The sentence of death has been passed upon us all. But Jesus, the Holy Son of God, "tasted death for every man." He became the "Ark" into whom, in the foreknowledge of God, every believer is placed. We are planted *into* Him upon His cross; and in Christ we are drawn out, like

Moses, from the waters of death—drawn out into a new life, as those who are "alive from the dead," having received the Spirit of adoption whereby we become sons and daughters of the Lord God Almighty.

Stephen tells us, in his brief history of the birth of Moses, that he was "fair in the sight of God" (Acts 7:20, margin); and as the Redeemer gazes upon the soul redeemed from destruction, and made a new creation in Himself, He says, "Thou art all fair, My love."

Upon our experiential knowledge of the beginning of this new life depends the extent of the "face-to-face" communion with God that we desire to know.

Have we really understood the "first principles of Christ" in the message of His cross?

Just as the babe Moses was placed in the ark and committed to the river, we, who as sinners are under sentence of death, are placed into Jesus Christ upon His cross. Henceforth we are to look at ourselves as God looks at us: planted into Christ and crucified with Him; redeemed from destruction, and, in the Ark Christ Jesus, carried out of the old life into the new, to walk in newness of life.

It is all one message throughout the Scriptures, repeated in various forms again and again—God using history and type to foreshadow the meaning of Calvary.

The flood in the days of Noah pictures the judgment and death of the old creation under the curse of God, and tells of the souls borne in an ark to a new world and a new life.

Israel crossing Jordan out of the wilderness life into the new life in Canaan, with the "ark" standing in the midst of the river until "all the people were passed over," bears the same message. These and many other incidents all point to Calvary, where the waters of death swept over the Son of God, and we, as the accursed ones, died with Him.

When the daughter of Pharaoh saw the babe and took compassion on him, she called his name Moses—that is, "drawn out," or "saved from the water"; and "drawn out" was the characteristic of his whole life afterwards. He was *drawn out* of the waters of death, to be trained as a king's son. When he was grown up, he was *drawn out* by God from his worldly home and surroundings to a desert life alone with Him, and later on he was *drawn out* from his seclusion to be God's instrument for leading Israel out of Egypt. He was afterwards *drawn out* from the active work of the camp to the Mount of God, for closer fellowship with Him, and finally was *drawn out* of the world altogether into the bosom of the Eternal.

We have seen that for a little while the

babe Moses was given back to the old home
and the old keeping. It is even so with us.
We have passed out of death into life, and
become children of God; but for a little
season we are left in the old surroundings
because we are babes, and because the
time is not yet ripe for us to know our high
calling and the discipline needed for the
heirs of God. The Father waits for His babes
until they are weaned and able to bear the
detaching from things necessary at first. "I
taught Ephraim also to go, taking them by
their arms" (Hosea 11:3), said God about
Israel. In God's time, and by His own ten-
der dealing, the soul must be weaned and
taught to walk alone, even though it means
many tears. At last, like a sobbing infant, it
sinks to rest in the will of God and says,
"Surely I have stilled and quieted my soul;
like a weaned child with his mother, like a
weaned child is my soul within me" (Psalm
131:2, *ASV*).

*"And the child grew, and she brought him
unto Pharaoh's daughter, and he became
her son"* (Exodus 2:10). Moses was taken
from his mother's hands and placed in the
care of a stranger, who brought him up as
her own son; then he was left in Pharaoh's
court for nearly forty years. At the close of
this time it is written of him that he "was
learned in all the wisdom of the Egyptians,
and was mighty in words and in deeds"

(Acts 7:22). "The heir, as long as he is a child, differeth nothing from a servant, though he be lord of all; but is under tutors and governors until the time appointed of the father" (Galatians 4:1–2). Many of God's children chafe over the long years of training, they know not for what cause. They are weary of the "instruction" in all the "wisdom of the Egyptians," and long to throw themselves into the service of God. But the pattern Son waited thirty years in the village of Nazareth before He went forth for the brief service of three years.

The souls who are yet "under tutors and governors" need sorely to learn how to wait for God and rest in His will. Let us remember that circumstances are planned of God to fit us for the calling He has in view for us, in the economy of His grace. Let us wait until we know His pattern for our life, lest, in our impatience, we throw aside the very things permitted by Him to fit us for some special service in His vineyard.

CHAPTER 2

THE CRISIS AND THE CROSS

"By faith Moses . . . refused to be called the son of Pharaoh's daughter, choosing rather to suffer affliction with the people of God than to enjoy the pleasures of sin for a season, esteeming the reproach of Christ greater riches . . . for he had respect unto the recompense of the reward" (Hebrews 11:24–26).

IN the fullness of God's time there came a crisis in the life of Moses, and his decision then may be said to lie at the very foundation of that "face-to-face" friendship with God which he afterwards enjoyed. Up to that time God had been guiding his life almost unconscious to him. Dormant in his memory might lie thoughts of early days . . . but his path may have seemed quite clear and without anything in it to indicate an impending change, until, in the purpose of God, it was necessary for Moses himself to intelligently co-operate with Him.

God had chosen Moses, but now the time

had come when Moses must choose God.
We are not told how the crisis came about;
we only know the outcome, and that the
power that enabled him to act was faith—
faith in his mother's God, for Jochebed
must have taught her boy of Him in whom
she trusted. It was faith that came from
calm and quiet consideration, for we are
told that he "looked unto the recompense
of the reward" (*ASV*): literally, *"he looked
beyond"* or *"away from that which was before his eyes"* (*Conybeare*). He was brought
to consider his position in the light of eternity, and to make a choice as to whether he
would live for present or for future gain.

He found himself surrounded by all that
one's heart could wish. "Mighty in word
and deed," he was honored and powerful.
Tradition declares that he was a successful
commander-in-chief of the Egyptian army;
and it has been pointed out that he could
not have marshaled the host of the Israelites as he did without military skill of an
advanced kind. In any case, a great future
lay before him as the adopted son of
Pharaoh's daughter. But his eyes were open
to see that there was a "beyond" to this
present world, and a "reward." He faced it
all, counted the cost, looked away from all
that was before his eyes, and made his
choice to live for eternity and God. His
choice involved a refusal that would mean

a great loss so far as this world was concerned. The "pleasures" and "treasures" of Egypt were all within his grasp, but with his eyes on the future he surrendered the present gain, took his stand, and "*refused* to be called the son of Pharaoh's daughter."

Some such crisis must come to each of us, when the heavenly vision of the high calling of God in Christ Jesus breaks upon us. We are children of the heavenly King, but, as it were, under tutors and governors until the time appointed by the Father. We have been left by Him in circumstances and surroundings that seem entirely of this world, while, unknown to us, He has been training mind and character for future service. Then the time comes when, as joint-heirs with Christ, we must know our high and holy calling—the "upward calling of God in Christ Jesus"—and deliberately choose the path of the cross, that we may be perfected as our Master; for it is written of Him: "Though He were a Son, yet learned He obedience by the things which He suffered" (Hebrews 5:8). We are "heirs of God, and joint-heirs with Christ; if so be that we suffer with Him, that we may be also glorified together" (Romans 8:17).

We are distinctly told that it was by "faith" Moses was able to choose "affliction" instead of "pleasures," "reproach" instead of "riches." "Faith is the giving substance to things hoped for, the *test* of things not seen" (Hebrews 11:1, *ASV*, margin).

Alas! over how many of the promises of God to us can it not be said, "The word preached did not profit them, because they were not united by faith to it" (Hebrews 4:2, margin)? Faith puts to the proof the statements of God by acting upon them, and in the acting finds their substance and reality. Faith tests the unseen things, and translates them into real experience.

This was strikingly true in the case of Moses. By faith he looked beyond the things before his eyes—he deliberately chose to refuse all the "pleasures" and "treasures" of the present; and faith tested, proved, or gave substance to his hopes. He was led step by step away from things seen, into a fellowship and communion with the unseen God of which he had no conception when he made his choice in Egypt.

"Faith" is the key to all the treasuries of God. The gospel is practically God's statement of what *is* in the spiritual world. Faith is simply believing God's word, however contrary it may appear to the things of sense and sight. Faith in God's statement to us is proved by action. We act according to what is told us by God, which we believe and must of necessity obey. Living faith involves action; without action it may be said to be dead, for a mental assent to the

truths of God will never give them substance in our lives. If we do believe God's
words we shall act according to those words.

We must not forget, however, that the
faith that is the "proving of things not seen"
demands direct communication with God.
Souls have often been shipwrecked here.
They have rested their faith upon the word
as spoken by *others*, rather than upon *God
Himself in His Word*.

The "faith" that can act as Moses did
must have the word of the Living God as its
basis—the declaration of the Living God
given in His written Word, but *by the Holy
Spirit applied as His direct word* to the soul.
When God speaks, His commands are His
enablings. By the faith wrought in us by
God, and the assurance of the reward of
knowing Him "face to face," we too can
refuse to be of the world and declare plainly
that we seek a better country, that is, a
heavenly; we too can refuse the pleasures
of sin and self-pleasing, and choose the
way of the cross; we too can hold lightly the
"treasures" that others clasp to their
breasts, and account reproach with Christ
as greater riches than them all. Faith accounting "reproach" as "riches" will give
substance to the accounting, and we shall
find that our light affliction, which is but
for the moment, works for us more and
more exceedingly an eternal weight of glory.

It is said that Moses surrendered the "pleasures of sin." We may have thought of these only as the pleasures of the world, which we have laid aside; but may there not be just as much self-pleasing and self-seeking in our lives as Christians?

To Moses these pleasures were in the court of Egypt: its treasures, intellectual companionship, cultured surroundings. How we admire him for his surrender, and think that we too would have done the same! But what about ourselves? Are we choosing comfort, *or the way of the cross?* The path of ease, *or the way of sacrifice?* Are we shirking suffering, or *choosing affliction for Christ's sake?* Are we compromising with the world, *or refusing to be identified with it?* Are we grasping the treasures of earth, or providing ourselves bags which wax not old, a treasure in the heavens that faileth not?

Like Moses shall we turn from all the things that are before our eyes and seek to know the face of our God? Shall we determine by His grace that we will know Him in the closest intimacy that is possible while on earth?

CHAPTER 3

SELF-ENERGY AND FAILURE

"It came into his heart to visit his brethren. . . . And seeing one of them suffer wrong, he defended him" (Acts 7:23–24).

MOSES had made his choice. Does this make him ready to be a vessel unto honor fit for the Master's use? Not yet!—surrender to God, and choosing the path of the cross, is not all. The conflict we have gone through in making the choice, and the wondrous peace that fills our hearts when that choice is made, may make it appear as if the needed work is done; but in reality it is only the beginning of our training, for only from the central throne of the will of a really conquered soul can God work out His deepest purposes.

Moses did not yet know himself! Instruction in all the wisdom of this world, and might in word and deed, are not enough preparation for an effective instrument in the hand of God.

Alas, alas!—that in the dispensation of the Holy Spirit we should know no better than Moses! In our reliance upon the wisdom of Egypt, upon oratory and fleshly energy, we act still as if the weapons of our warfare must be carnal, and go forth, as Moses did, to find out our sad mistake.

The great inward crisis in his life, when impelled to make a definite choice as to his future course, was followed by events that, in the overruling of God, freed him from the life he had decided to renounce.

It is always so when we are in line with God. His inward dealings co-operate with His exterior workings to effect His will. If God deals deeply with us to bring us inwardly to choose the path of the cross, it will not be long before we shall find ourselves, unexpectedly perhaps, in circumstances where our heart's choice is translated into fact. Maybe by some act of our own, some apparent failure or mistake, but suddenly—all is changed.

"It came into his heart to visit his brethren." Thus simply does Stephen speak of a step which had momentous consequences. It was first a thought, then action, and unforeseen results.

Moses *"went out unto his brethren, and looked"* (Exodus 2:11). Had he never looked before? He must have known that he was of their race. In all these long years when he passed as son of Pharaoh's daughter, and shared in all the pleasures of Egypt, had he forgotten the people of God and their burdens? Or did he remember and push the thoughts away? The decision that he had now come to, that he would cast in his lot with them, could not have been the work of a moment, but was probably the result of deep heart-searching before the God whom he knew had spared his life when so many innocent babes had been swept away.

Moses *looked*, and his heart was stirred! We gather from the words of Stephen that Moses already knew that he was to be the deliverer of Israel, and so when he went out to visit his brethren, and saw one of them suffering wrong, he defended him, smiting the Egyptian. Ah, Moses, Moses, this is the way of Egypt, but not of God!

This reminds us of Peter drawing his sword to defend the Son of God, who needed but to speak and have legions of angels to protect Him. It describes too many who are fighting for God today, drawing their swords and smiting all that they conceive to be wrong, forgetting that the Master said, "All they that take the sword shall perish with the sword," and again, "If My kingdom were of this world, then would My servants fight." That His servants do fight shows their forgetfulness of the way of the cross and the spirit of their Lord.

Israel would never have been delivered if deliverance depended upon Moses smiting the Egyptians one by one. God had a far better way than this. How small and narrow is our vision! If we would but give ourselves up to God, and seek first to know Him and His will, He would then accomplish great things by us.

God meant to save Israel by the hand of Moses, but *not* in Moses' way. Moses himself was the greatest difficulty; it would take time and patient training to make this fiery man a polished shaft.

God had to teach Moses first by failure. He *supposed* that his brethren would have understood that *God* was giving them deliverance! Probably they would have understood if the means had been of God; but this was not God's way, so how could God bear witness to it!

We are amazed when the souls we want to help do not accept us. We know that God has called us, and told us that He will give deliverance to souls by our hands. With hearts full of our secret dealings with Him, and of all that He has said to us, we go out and *suppose* that others will understand that God is working through us, when as yet it is not God at all! It *is* God, in so far as that He permits our efforts to be made, but only that we may fail and know ourselves.

The record in Exodus tells us that after

Moses had "looked this way and that way . . . he slew the Egyptian, and hid him in the sand" (Exodus 2:12). This was not "worthy of God." He does not do His work like this, nor ask His children to do anything unbefitting their high and heavenly calling. When He did bring out Israel from Egypt, it was by a stretched-forth arm and glorious power, so that the Egyptians themselves bowed down and said, "Get thee out."

Let us not dare to put God's name to anything that needs a "looking this way and that" before or after it is done. Let us beware of any money-getting in His name, or even attempted soul-getting, that cannot bear the light of His scrutiny.

Surely Moses must have been conscious that all was not right! When he retired to rest that night, did it not occur to him that Israel would never be delivered in such a way? So, too, does it not dawn upon us that, in spite of all our "defending and avenging," souls are yet in bondage to sin and the world, and that our puny efforts to free them are like an attempt to empty the ocean with a spoon? Some know it, and are almost crushed. They say, "Are we then to do nothing when we see the burdens of the oppressed?" In God's name, Yes; but let us *first* get into line with God, so as to work with Him, and not apart from Him.

God and Moses can bring Israel out of

Egypt, but Moses alone—never!

"And when he went out the second day, behold, two men of the Hebrews strove together; and he said to him that did the wrong, Wherefore smitest thou thy fellow? And he said, *Who made thee a prince and a judge over us? Intendest thou to kill me, as thou killedst the Egyptian? And Moses feared*" (Exodus 2:13–14). It was one of those shafts that strike home, winged by the hand of God! It is hard to be told the truth so sharply, and by those you seek to help. Unpleasant though it may be, if we are open to these home-thrusts from others, who see us as we cannot see ourselves, we will be able to submit our lives to Him who can adjust them so that they give no occasion of reproach. No soul that shuts itself up within itself, and carefully avoids every outlook but its own, will ever "look from the top" with God over a wide horizon.

So *this* was how the thing looked to the very men he longed to help! If Moses had been able to justify his action to himself, it was a rough awakening. The man he rebuked for smiting his brother could not distinguish between his own action and that of Moses! In one case, true, it was a common quarrel; in the other it was the noble ideal of delivering the oppressed. The ignorant Hebrew surely could not distinguish things that differ!

No, no, child of God, that action of yours may be prompted by a noble ideal, but to others looking on it savors of the world, or of the spirit of the flesh. We ought not let our good be evil spoken of, and we are bidden to avoid the *appearance* of evil, and to take thought for things honorable in the sight of all men.

"Who made thee a judge over us?" met the ears of Moses as he sought to make peace between his brethren. What utter failure! Let us thank God for our failures and our rude awakenings. Far, far better to have them now than to live in self-delusion and awaken too late, to find at the judgment seat that we must "suffer loss" because we could not bear the truth.

The shaft struck home. Moses feared, and Moses fled—fled to the land of Midian, a pilgrim and a stranger. He had made his choice, and by his own free will determined to take the path of the cross—to suffer affliction, loss, and reproach. Now in two brief days, and apparently by his own folly, his court life had faded into the past, and he found himself a wanderer and alone, a stranger in a strange land.

This period in the history of Moses has its counterpart in our own experience; but, alas, many of us spend years in learning our powerlessness in the work of God, although we know that we are not acceptable to the souls we want to help, and "Who put you over us?" not unfrequently meets our ears. Let us not *blame the people,* as we are so often disposed to do, but rather let us seek the light of God to know the cause of failure in ourselves, that He may make us vessels unto honor, fit for His use.

CHAPTER 4

THE FLAME OF FIRE

"The angel of the LORD appeared unto him in a flame of fire out of the midst of a bush" (Exodus 3:2).

GOD had made ready for Moses in the land of Midian. His steps were ordered of the Lord, and he was guided to a place where his bread would be given him, and his water would be sure. Severed from the magnificent surroundings of the palace of Pharaoh and the pleasures of the highly civilized capital of Egypt, Moses was given the joys of a quiet home, and taught to be content with simple food and a pastoral life in a strange land.

Through Stephen's narrative we learn that Moses spent forty years in retirement in Midian. Forty years is a long period of life now, and God does not take as much time to prepare His instruments in these days.

As Moses led the sheep year after year,

did he ever think that God had forgotten that transaction with Himself when he looked beyond to the reward, and chose the pathway of the cross? Or did he have many sore conflicts over the thought that he had frustrated the grace of God, and been put aside as a marred vessel? Did he ever say to himself that by his own folly and self-will he had cut himself off from the people he had longed to help?

We are given no trace of Moses' thoughts during these forty years, but it is probable that God waited until every hope of his being sent back to become the deliverer of his oppressed brethren faded away.

God waited for Moses until, in the silence of the desert, his whole being was stilled and all "creaturely activity" and hurry and impulse had died away.

Oh, how restive we are in ourselves! How we dislike being still, especially when everything around us seems to be moving at greatest speed. Yes, the Church of God has caught the fever of the world! But God has yet His hidden ones, the "quiet in the land" (Psalm 35:20).

Maybe, child of God, you have found your desert training in some workroom or kitchen, at some lonely post on the mission field, or in some worldly home in your own country. You have been agonizing, struggling, wondering when God will set you free. You once thought He meant to do great things by you, but you have been so hedged in that all hope has died away, all plans and schemes are gone. At last you are content to "feed the flock," and to be faithful to Him in that which is least. "Alas! Here am I, occupied with nothing but the things of earth, and God's world seems to be needing me. Am I never to be among those privileged to undo the bands of the yoke and let the oppressed go free?" Oh, child of God, your Father never forgets, and His clocks are never behind time. Wait! "But I have waited many years!" Your Father knows—lie down in His will, and be at rest; don't you know that His will is more than His work, and that your Lord has said, "Whosoever shall do the will of My Father, . . . he is My brother, and sister, and mother"? The waiting must needs be. The aim and the end of all His work in us is to teach us to "prove what is that good, and acceptable, and perfect will of God."

In God's dealings with Moses, the time came when His purposes matured—the instrument and the people were ready.

The king of Egypt had died—the king who had known Moses in his youth—and the people of Israel were groaning under their bondage. "God heard their groaning, and God remembered His covenant with Abraham" (Exodus 2:24). Not that God had

ever forgotten, but the conditions necessary for His working had to be fulfilled.

The mystery of the manifestation of divine power depending upon our human co-
operation has ever been strange to finite
creatures. It lies mainly in the freedom of
will that belongs to us. God cannot deliver
us from bondage unless we desire Him to;
therefore He must permit pressure to come
upon us in one way or another, so as to
bring us to the point of asking Him to do
for us what He has been ready and able to
do all the time.

Israel needed to come to the point of
groaning for deliverance before God could
set them free; and the Lord brought them
to this position by permitting their bondage
and suffering to increase until they sighed
and cried to the God who was only waiting
to save. The instrument was ready. The
deliverer was being prepared. How little Israel knew it! In their anguish and sorrow
they seemed forsaken by God and man.

Is it not just so today? Our God is the
same God. As we see Him slowly and silently maturing His plan for the deliverance
of Israel, and marvel at the beauty of His
working which this has unveiled to us, even
so is He now perfecting His plans for the
translation of His called-out ones, the
Church of the first-born enrolled in heaven.

If we will abide in the secret place of the

Most High, and look with Him "from the top," we shall stand in His counsel, and discern the signs of the times that point to the Lord's appearing.

With Israel ready, Moses can be told that God's purposes are ripe for fulfillment. God's way of dealing with him is full of significance. He meets Moses as, in the ordinary path of duty, he takes the sheep to their pasture on the mount. If we are longing to be used by God, we may be sure that "doing the next thing" in the daily round is the best training for service. We shall then be ready for God's call when *He* is ready to use us.

He arrested the attention of Moses by a flame of fire burning in a common little bush, and the strange thing about it was that the bush continued to burn and yet was not consumed.

Moses said, "I will now turn aside and see this great sight, why the bush is not burnt" (Exodus 3:3). A bush on fire with no human hand to set it alight, no fuel to keep it burning. It was just a picture to Moses of what God could do with him, and a picture to the people of God for all time of the grace of Him who is willing to dwell in human beings as lowly and insignificant as the little thornbush on the Mount of Horeb.

God spoke to Moses out of that bush, as He has spoken to many of us. He called him by his name; for God's messages are ever personal and direct, so that we need not anyone else to say, "Thou art the man." When God speaks, we forget our neighbors, and we know whom He means.

But Moses needs to know how solemn a thing it is to meet God, even though it be not yet "face to face"! Moses, *the place whereon thou standest is holy ground."* Holy ground!—though a moment before it was but common land. Holy ground because of the holy presence of the God of glory.

"If any man defile the temple of God, him shall God destroy; for the temple of God is holy, which temple ye are" (1 Corinthians 3:17). Oh, how deeply we need to remember this! Our inquiry then would not be, "Is there any harm in this or that?" but, "Is it befitting the temple of God?" If God dwells in us as He dwelt in the bush, then surely His sacred presence should make even common things alight with the glory of heaven.

"Moreover He said, I am . . . GOD" (Exodus 3:6). The same God that Abraham knew, when he fell upon his face while He talked with him. The God that Isaac and Jacob also knew. "I am . . . GOD." "And Moses hid his face; for he was afraid." It was not the time for "face-to-face" friendship yet!

Then "the LORD said, I have surely seen the affliction of My people, . . . and have heard their cry. . . . I know their sorrows; and I am come down to deliver" (Exodus 3:7–8). "I am God, . . . and I am come to deliver." Jehovah, the great "I AM"—for God is an eternal NOW. His heart towards souls in affliction and sorrow is the same now as when He revealed Himself to Moses. He is immutable, without a shadow of turning.

Oh, how we need so to meet with God that He can open His heart to us and show us His love and compassion to this poor lost world, the love that gave His only begotten Son for its salvation! Who shall ever fathom the love of the cross? The love of the Father in yielding His Son to death, the love of the Son in consenting to be separated from His Father through the cross, and the love of the Eternal Spirit who yearns over the redeemed ones now with jealous envy.

"Come now, therefore, and I will send thee . . . that thou mayest bring forth My people" (Exodus 3:10). Does God want Moses in partnership? "*I* am come down to deliver" (verse 8). Jehovah had revealed to him first Himself, "I am . . . God"; then His heart, "I have seen, I am come"; and now He reveals to him His plans for accomplishing the deliverance. God by the hand of Moses! Not Moses with the help of God!

Only by such a meeting with God can effectual service for Him begin. We must receive our commission direct from Him, lest we run before we are sent and merit the words spoken by Jehovah to the prophets of Israel in later years, "I have not sent these prophets, yet they ran. I have not spoken to them, yet they prophesied. . . . Behold, I am against the prophets . . . that use their tongues, and say, He saith" (Jeremiah 23:21–31).

CHAPTER 5

SELF-DIFFIDENCE AND LOSS

"And Moses said unto God, Who am I, that I should go? . . . What shall I say? . . . But, behold, they will not believe me" (Exodus 3:11,13; 4:1).

WHAT a change in Moses! How ready he was to go forty years before! But now he shrinks back. *"I? Who am I, that I should go?"* All the self-sufficiency gone. Is this the man who was mighty in words and works?

The colloquy between God and His shrinking servant has been repeated again and again in many hearts today. For one thing, the task was a stupendous one! What would it mean? What would God do with him? Moses had looked upon the burdens of his oppressed brethren, and he knew the tyranny of Pharaoh and what it meant to have him as an enemy. *To be sent to deliver*

Israel! The sketch that God had drawn out as to His plan of operations looked simply impossible. Bring them up out of Egypt into a good land now occupied by other nations!—and he, one man, with no resources, no influence, no means, no co-worker! Impossible!

But God can do impossible things! It matters not how great the scheme if God draws it out; it matters not how insurmountable the difficulties appear, if God undertakes the responsibility.

Moses does not venture to question the scheme, but he does question his fitness to take part in it, so he shrinks back with objection after objection. "*I go to Pharaoh?*" But *"I will be with thee,"* answers Jehovah.

An ambassador from the King of kings will have his Master's authority at his back. Moses would not be sent in his own personal capacity, nor even as the man who once was a royal prince in the land. God had allowed sufficient time to elapse for all that to die away. He wanted none of earth's influence for His chosen messenger, nor personal power from position. There must be no fear of this intruding now. Moses must go in the authority and power of God alone.

But *"when I come unto the children of Israel, and shall say, . . . God . . . hath sent me unto you; and they shall say to me, What is His name? what shall I say?"* (Exodus 3:13).

The patient Lord has much trouble with this shrinking man; but He tenderly meets his fears, and answers every difficulty. He was to tell the oppressed Israelites just what God had told him—the God of their fathers had appeared to him and sent him unto them. He was told exactly what to do; was promised a hearing; and was fore-warned that the steps he was bidden to take would not be successful at first—but that God would work for His people, and eventually they would be allowed to come away; not empty, either, like slaves stealing away, but they would come out of Egypt in the sight of all the people, actually has-tened by them, and loaded with their gifts!

Whatever God undertakes He carries out royally in the face of all men. Israel would have been only too glad to get away from their taskmasters in *any* condition; but when God leads forth His people it shall be in triumph, by a mighty hand and by a stretched-out arm.

If we, His children, when we get into tangled corners, even by our own folly and sometimes wrongdoing, would only turn to God as a King and a Father, and cast our-selves upon Him, He would work for us, and lead us out of our troubles safely and in a way worthy of a royal King.

Jehovah has dealt with two of Moses' difficulties, but Moses is not yet satisfied.

He cannot reconcile himself to the prospect of such an undertaking; he has rather unpleasant memories of a certain day when one of these very Hebrews, to whom God wants to send him, turned round upon him saying, "Who made thee a ruler over *us?*"

The adversary keeps these memories for sensitive souls, and he knows how to bring them up in critical moments. The shaft had pierced deep into the mind of the fiery and sensitive man, whose attempt to avenge and defend his oppressed brethren had cost him so much.

The greater the cost and the sacrifice in going forth to the aid of others, the deeper the wound when that aid is rejected. Only keenly sensitive natures can understand the suffering that Moses must have experienced when his hopes were dashed to the ground and he fled from Egypt in terror.

To be sent back to the people who had rejected him! Does the bitter memory of that slain Egyptian, and the undignified hiding in the sand, rankle in Moses' mind? Is he afraid the taunt will be repeated, and the terror come back, so that he must flee again? How ashamed he is when he thinks about it. In the sight of God his motive was pure, but he never can forgive himself for his folly.

How the devil haunts God's children with memories like these! Paul, at the very end of his life, could not forget that he had once persecuted the Church of God, and had actually given his vote for the innocent ones to be put to death. "It is God that justifieth; who is he that condemneth? It is Christ Jesus that died, yea rather, that was raised from the dead" (Romans 8:33–34, *ASV*). "It is Christ Jesus that died" is the answer to all the past for Paul, and for all who shelter under the blood of the slain Lamb.

Moses speaks again: *"But, behold, they will not believe me; . . . they will say, The LORD hath not appeared"* (Exodus 4:1). Moses had *supposed* once they would understand that God would deliver them by his hand; and the error then made him fear to risk disappointment now. Suppositions are not enough; we must have certainties . . . and Moses will find it very different when God really sends him.

God answers this fear by showing him His power, and proving to him that He will bear him witness in the eyes of those to whom he is sent.

In a picture-lesson God teaches him that He only needs a rod to fulfill His purposes. He bids Moses cast the rod held in his hand upon the ground, and it becomes a serpent. He bids him lay hold of the serpent by the tail, and it becomes a rod.

Unconscious preparation for Egypt! He will have to meet the magicians, and he must first have proved God's power, so that in calm fearlessness he can face them and conquer.

Again we meet with the need of "faith" as the one thing to link nothingness with Omnipotence: "If ye have faith . . . nothing shall be impossible unto you," and again, "Have the faith of God. Whosoever shall say unto this mountain, Be thou removed, . . . and shall not doubt in his heart, . . . *he shall have whatsoever he saith*" (Mark 11:22–23, margin). Moses must not be left with one shadow of doubt in his heart, so that the things that he "saith" at God's command shall be done.

God will take the same trouble today to train His children to have absolute unwavering faith in the weapon put into our hands: the sword of the Spirit—the Word of God, which is mighty to the pulling down of strongholds.

"And Moses said unto the LORD, *O my Lord, I am not eloquent* [a "man of words"], *neither heretofore nor since Thou hast spoken unto Thy servant; but I am slow of speech, and of a slow tongue"* (Exodus 4:10).

Now it is all out! First, "Who am I?" I have no position, no influence, no authority! Second, "They will not believe me." They did not do so once, and I do not care to try again. And, thirdly, "I am not eloquent." Perhaps Moses said to himself, "Forty years in the wilderness has taken away my flow of language. Once I was mighty in words, but not now; I have become a man of few words, slow of speech and tongue."

If Moses only knew it, this was his best preparation. Eloquence is more often a hindrance than an advantage. When God speaks, He speaks little, but what He says is done. With Him speaking is doing, and one word will accomplish His purpose. When God wants a man to be His mouthpiece, He sometimes chooses one who is not eloquent, and has no language of his own, so that God may speak through him.

Paul clearly understood this when he wrote, "Not with wisdom of words, lest the cross of Christ should be made of none effect" (1 Corinthians 1:17). It is made of none effect, alas! by the flowery language in which it is too often clothed. God forgive us for wreathing the cross with flowers—even flowers of speech, as well as of thought. It needs its intense reality to fulfill its work, even as in all its awful power it shook Jerusalem that eventful day when the horror of a great darkness was over the land.

The Lord's answer to Moses was decisive. He had made his mouth. It was enough. The God who made his mouth could open his mouth, and teach him what to say. "Go, and I will be with thy mouth." This concludes the matter: every difficulty is met—

position, people, power, language—what more is needed?

But the heart of Moses faints! Yes, it is all true: the path is clear; there is no question about the call, the command, the equipment, the power; he has only to give himself up to God, like that rod in his hand, and God will do the rest. There is nothing lacking now but his free, glad consent to be God's instrument—and God waits. But his heart fails him; he cannot face the work. The Lord has been so gracious in listening to his fears that he does not dare refuse—so, with almost a gasp of terror, he says, "O my Lord, send, I pray Thee, by the hand of him whom Thou wilt send" (Exodus 4:13); as much as to say, "Thou must have Thy way, Lord, and if I must go, well—but I'd rather not!"—a most ungracious, unwilling assent.

God cannot fulfill His deepest purposes through us unless there is hearty, unhesitating co-operation with Him, for an unwilling instrument cannot exercise the needed "faith," and faith is the capacity, or channel, through which the divine power works. The shrinking does not hinder if there is the full response of the will. Moses did not *refuse* to go; he agreed to yield to the divine will, but his faith could not reach to the point where God could use his mouth and give him power of utterance.

It is written that "the anger of the LORD

was kindled against Moses." He was grieved, and may we venture to say, disappointed? He had intended to do all through Moses, but the latter's shrinking and ungracious assent to the service that he was called to made it necessary that He should use another vessel with him. If Moses had not faith that God would give him the words needed, then God could not make him His mouthpiece.

The Almighty God stands powerless before unbelief, and He can be limited by our lack of faith in His purposes of grace towards us.

It was not an erratic or a petulant change, this determination to give Aaron as a spokesman to Moses. The action was governed by the law that surrender and faith are the only conditions in which God can work in human vessels.

Aaron was given to Moses to be his spokesman, or, as the Lord Himself expressed it, "instead of a mouth." And Moses lost his opportunity of proving what God could do. He took, shall we say, God's second best instead of His best! He yielded to his fears instead of believing that God could do for him the "impossible" thing. Moses had to later regret his fainting heart this day, for he made for himself, through Aaron, difficulties that need never have come in his path.

Are we not doing the same thing day after day? Let us *never* look at the human side, and, because our hearts fail us, choose God's second best.

But if we shrink now from some purpose of God, He will bring us back to it sooner or later. Many years afterwards, when Aaron had died, Moses knew God better, and his tongue was loosed. At the close of his life, he spoke a parting "song" in the ears of Israel (Deuteronomy 32:1–43)—perhaps as a preparation for the "new song" he was so soon to sing, "the song of Moses . . . and the song of the Lamb" (Revelation 15:3).

The interview was over. Moses now goes to Jethro, and he breaks to him the news that he must return to Egypt. He says nothing of all that had passed on the mountainside. Souls who have had interviews like these are not disposed to talk much about them; neither does God reveal Himself often in such a way, until the soul has learned to walk silently with Him.

CHAPTER 6

THE FAITHFUL SERVANT

"Moses indeed was faithful in all His house ['*God's house,*' margin] *as a servant"* (Hebrews 3:5, *ASV*).

WE need not trace the steps of Moses as he returned to the land of Egypt, other than to note one incident on the journey thither.

God seems to have given no definite directions as to His will concerning Moses' wife and little ones in the path that lay before him. We read only that he took his family with him on the journey. Perhaps as "a matter of course"! But God will not have His will taken for granted; and He has to let us find out, sometimes rather sorely, that we have never sought His mind about a particular step, so quickly and so instinctively do we run our own way. The life of real dependence upon God every moment is not an easy one to learn. He could have said to Moses, "Go, *take thy family,* and return to Egypt"—but He did not.

The Lord permitted Moses to start on his journey, together with his family, but when they rested at an inn, we are told, "the LORD met him, and sought to kill him" (Exodus 4:24). He had evidently failed in obedience to God's commands concerning circumcision, and had done so through the objections of Zipporah his wife. But the faithful God could not overlook one single deviation from His will, and lays His hand upon Moses so unmistakably that his wife was forced to recognize the cause and yield the disputed point, and his life was spared.

This sharp discipline seems to have shown Moses that he must go alone into Egypt, for Zipporah evidently could not enter into the solemn conflict which lay before him with the powers of this world, behind whom were the powers of darkness. The bitter words she used showed clearly how she might embarrass him in his mission to Israel; so he sends his family back to the care of Jethro for a time, and forward to the unknown goes the lonely man.

One step at a time!—sufficient for the day. Moses did not think of all this when he stood before the Lord. Aaron now meets him on the way, sent by God, and together they go to the elders of Israel and begin their mission. "And the people believed!"—

and God so bare witness to all that He had promised that they not only believed but "bowed their heads and worshipped."

Passing over the details of the wondrous story of how God worked out His deliverance for Israel, let us briefly consider the main characteristics of Moses' walk with God from this time forward.

1. *His absolute, implicit obedience to God.* He did exactly what God told him to do, and no more. Again and again to God he went, sorely tried with the first results of his mission, until at last the conflict of faith grew too keen for him to bear, and he said, "Lord, . . . why is it that Thou hast sent me? For since I came to Pharaoh to speak in Thy name, he hath done evil to this people; *neither hast Thou delivered Thy people at all*" (Exodus 5:22–23).

It was a severe test, and if he had not had behind him such an interview with God, such an unqualified, unmistakable commission, such a knowledge of His will, his heart would have failed him. But Moses is going on "from faith to faith," and faith grows by testing. Only thus can it be developed and matured, until it can believe against hope and cry in the face of every obstacle, "It shall be done."

God now gives him a fresh and more explicit message for the oppressed people, with seven "I wills" enclosed in the Alpha and Omega of "I am Jehovah" (Exodus 6:6–8). He was known to Abraham, Isaac and Jacob, as "El-Shaddai," the Pourer-forth of blessing, but now He will reveal Himself to Israel as Jehovah, the Righteous God who must judge sin because He is the Just and Holy One.

Back to the stricken Israelites Moses goes with this Magna Carta of promised deliverance, but the people were in such anguish that they could not listen; they were too overwhelmed with their sorrow to pay attention. What can be done now? How can souls be lifted up when they are too crushed to heed? Surely God had let it go too far! Moses' heart must have been wrung with anguish. To be sent of God to deliver, and to be the very means of plunging the souls he had come to help into deeper suffering—it called for faith to trust through this: even the same faith that Jesus had in His Father, when He heard that Lazarus was sick, and yet abode two days in the place where He was.

It is in truth "the fellowship of His sufferings" when we must stand back and wait for His hour to come; wait for His permission to move, or to speak; wait and watch the fiery furnace grow still more heated, knowing that the sufferers reproach you for carrying a message from God which spoke of deliverance but which instead has apparently only placed them in the fires. Ah, this is sorrow indeed! But only thus can we learn fellowship with the afflictions of Christ, as with Him we wait and watch; like Him to be deeply distressed and troubled, as He was at the tomb of Lazarus, even though we know that our stricken one shall yet hear His voice and come forth to a new life in the power of His resurrection.

Moses suffered for these afflicted souls as he had never done in the early days, when, moved and stirred by looking on their burdens until his fiery indignation burst out, he smote the Egyptian. This deep, silent man had now a capacity for suffering that he had not then. Oh, the anguish in his voice as he cried to his Lord, "Neither hast Thou delivered Thy people at all." The cruel bondage of oppressed Israel had clouded his heart, and when the Lord bids him go again to Pharaoh he is depressed and disheartened, and replies, "Behold, the children of Israel have not hearkened unto me; how then shall Pharaoh hear me?" (Exodus 6:12).

Jehovah takes no notice of this passing cloud, but simply bids him go to Pharaoh and says that He will make him as "God" to him, with Aaron as his prophet. That is, that he shall be clothed with all the power and authority of God, and stand in His stead before the heathen king.

After this we get the constant refrain, *"As the LORD commanded them, so did they"* (Exodus 7:6, etc.). Step by step they had but to obey; and we watch these two men quietly, faithfully following each direction given them by God. How their faith increased as God bore witness to each step! The first manifestation of His power was the turning of the rod into a serpent, as Moses had seen it done once before; and then from this point, from faith to faith, the wonders grew.

What could not God do with that little rod! It was the medium of power in the first three judgments God sent upon Pharaoh. Then Moses is bidden simply to say, "Thus saith the LORD," and God bore witness to the word without using the rod. *Had Moses begun to lean upon IT somehow?*

God will not have us lean upon even the things He has given us, or used in the past; and it requires His ceaseless watching to keep us from clinging to, or resting upon, anything outside of Himself and His bare word. It will be so to the very end, and this accounts for many of His strange dealings with us. The things He gives must be returned, and given and returned again, so that we may be kept free and pliable for Him to do with us as He wills.

We must also be freed from rigid conceptions of His method of working. He used

the rod in the first miracles, then He shows
Moses that He can also work without the
rod, for nothing is necessary to Him. The
next miracles were performed by the word
of Jehovah through Moses. The swarms of
flies came after the word, "Thus saith the
LORD, . . . *Tomorrow shall this sign be*" (Exodus 8:20–23). Again, before the plague on
the livestock Moses said, "Thus saith the
LORD, . . . *There shall be* a very grievous
murrain" (Exodus 9:1–3)—and it was so.

Again God changes His methods: the
sixth plague was brought about in a different way, and the rod was used again. All
this taught Moses to be very pliable in the
hand of God, and very obedient. It taught
him to go forward just one step at a time,
and to have no preconceptions as to how
God would work that day.

2. *His uncompromising faithfulness.* It
was absolutely necessary that he should
not depart one iota from what God had
said. Pharaoh parleyed and sought to com-
promise as the judgments fell upon him,
but Moses must not swerve. Had he yielded
one degree he would have failed the Lord,
and frustrated His purposed deliverance for
Israel. He did not dare to act for one moment
as an independent agent on God's behalf.

"Sacrifice to your God in the land," said
Pharaoh, and Moses might have said, "Why
not in the land? This is a great concession;

we cannot expect more." But no, God had said three days' journey out of Egypt, and three days' journey it must be.

"Go now, ye that are men," again said Pharaoh. No, God had said "all." Then "Go, . . . only let your flocks and your herds be stayed." No, "there shall not an hoof be left behind," said the uncompromising servant of God, who was faithful to Him who appointed him.

Never, never, until we, too, are faithful, and implicitly obedient to every word that God has said, shall we be led on to know "face-to-face" friendship with Him.

It is not a light thing to be called "a friend of God"! It doubtless cost Abraham many tears, and hours of conflict as "against hope" he "believed in hope" that God would fulfill His word. It cost Moses much to stand unflinchingly true to God in the face of Israel's sufferings and Pharaoh's parleying.

Face-to-face friendship with God in its fullest meaning is only given when the loyalty of the soul has been proved beyond question, and faith has survived every test.

3. *His ceaseless recognition of God's responsibility.* It has been said that perfect obedience brings perfect rest, if we have confidence in the one we are obeying. This is true, and is the reason why we should learn to know our God—so as to be sure that we know His will and that we are un-

der His entire control.

Moses knew the God he was obeying, and therefore he did not carry any of the responsibility nor question the issue of the conflict in which he was engaged with the rulers of this world. "Moses cried to the LORD" we read again and again, and as a result he so spoke that Pharaoh knew he had to deal with *God,* not Moses.

Would that we had learned thus to be God's ambassadors, and to be so self-effaced while delivering the message that the souls to whom we are sent know they have to deal with God, and not with His messengers. Alas, it is to be feared that many of us have scarcely learned the first elements of spiritual service! We are so occupied with our little part that we get between God and the souls He sends us to. Even more, we fear to say "Thus saith the LORD," because we have not learned how to know His mind.

Pharaoh knew, too, that when Moses "cried to the LORD" the thing was done! "What things soever ye *desire,* when ye pray, believe that ye receive them, and ye shall have." There could be no questioning in the mind of Moses as to whether or not his prayers were in the will of God. "O God, *if* it be Thy will, remove this plague" would not do in such circumstances. Moses was not told, in so many words, to pray for the removal of the judgment, yet we read that he said to Pharaoh, "I will spread abroad my hands unto the LORD; and the thunder *shall cease*," and—"the thunders and hail ceased" (Exodus 9:29, 33)!

Ignorance of God and of His heart and His written Word lie at the bottom of much aimless prayer. How can we say "if it be Thy will" when He has plainly revealed His will as to much that we ask for? We need but to point Him to His Word, and say reverently, and with the boldness of faith, *"Do as Thou hast said."* He has yet to teach many of us, His children, the "prayer of faith," which *has* whatsoever it says because it asks in accordance with the will of God. We ourselves know not what we should pray for as we ought, but the Holy Spirit can give us that intuitive knowledge of His mind which comes from a close walk with Him.

As we read on in the record of the marvelous life of obedience and faith which sprang from that interview with God on Mount Horeb, the words "Moses cried to the LORD" meet us at every turn. When the people he had brought out through such suffering and conflict turned upon him, his resource was God. Boldly the faithful servant is permitted to speak to Jehovah, as again and again he throws back upon Him the responsibility of the fretful Hebrews.

4. *His fearlessness.* "By faith he forsook

Egypt, not fearing the wrath of the king; for he endured, as seeing Him who is invisible" (Hebrews 11:27). We are expressly told that the fearlessness of Moses sprang from faith, and the brief passage in Hebrews throws light on his whole history. Every step forward was the result of a faith that grew day by day as he endured its testing, and endured because he saw Him who is only visible to faith. "For he that cometh to God must believe that HE IS, and that He is a rewarder of them that diligently seek Him" (Hebrews 11:6). Moses forsook Egypt by faith—faith that God would see the thing through; faith that God would shield from the wrath of the king, and protect and provide for the great host of undisciplined, helpless souls He was leading out into the unknown wilderness.

God was becoming to Moses a greater reality than the "things that are seen," and bolder and bolder became his walk of faith, until the unseen grew more real and tangible to him than the visible. How could he fear the "wrath of the king" when he walked in fearless fellowship with the King of kings?

"By faith he kept the passover, and the sprinkling of the blood, that the destroyer of the firstborn should not touch them" (Hebrews 11:28, *ASV*). It was the faith of Moses that was the link with God's power on behalf of Israel. God had said that if the

lamb was killed and the blood sprinkled, the destroyer would not touch. Moses believed God, and "according to his faith" it was unto them. He had no fear when God's judgments were abroad, because they were sheltered under the blood of the slain lamb.

How wonderful his faith was! It was even greater than Abraham's. *He* had faith, first for himself and then for Isaac; but Moses had faith for the *deliverance of a nation.*

"By faith they passed through the Red Sea as by dry land: which the Egyptians assaying to do were swallowed up" (Hebrews 11:29, ASV). Moses had no fear of danger in passing through the Red Sea, for he obeyed God, and wielded the rod of His power, stretching out his hand over the sea. Faith that God would bear witness accompanied his actions, and by faith the work was made perfect—was brought to full fruition. The waters were divided, and Israel passed through as on dry land. They went through dangers that proved disastrous to the Egyptians when they tried to follow.

Ah! is it not so today? Faith can fearlessly walk a path that would be death without the word of the Living God. The Egyptians copied the walk of faith, and were drowned. No copy of living faith will stand the hour of testing. Let even the children of God take heed. Let them see that they dare not try to follow in the steps of others, without the command of God and the assurance of His presence in the way, or they must surely fail.

Oh faith, thou art in truth the proving of things hoped for, the evidence of things not seen! "If thou canst believe, all things are possible to him that believeth." Lord, increase our faith!

Lastly, let us note briefly the humility of Moses, as strikingly shown in his attitude toward Jethro when he came to him in the wilderness with Zipporah and his two sons. Moses tells him what God had done, and Jethro rejoices. Then, as he finds Moses engaged alone in seeking to settle the recurring disputes among the people, he suggests a plan whereby the work could be divided with others, adding, "If thou shalt do this thing, *and God command thee so,* then thou shalt be able to endure" (Exodus 18:23). Moses did not reject the counsel of Jethro because he had personally been guided by God hitherto, and the way in which he received the suggestion teaches us that the soul who has the most deeply learned to know God is ready to give others an attentive and respectful hearing.

We see, too, how real a link Jethro was in the chain of events that led Moses nearer and nearer to the Mount of "face-to-face" communion. How disorganized the camp would have been, when Moses had gone forty days aside with God, but for the wise advice of Jethro and the teachable spirit of Moses, the faithful servant of God.

CHAPTER 7

FROM GLORY TO GLORY

"The LORD said unto Moses, Come up to Me into the mount, . . . and Moses went up, . . . and a cloud covered the mount. And the glory of the LORD abode upon Mount Sinai" (Exodus 24:12, 15–16).

JEHOVAH Himself brought Israel out of Egypt, manifesting His presence "by day in a pillar of cloud, . . . by night in a pillar of fire." They had been led through stage after stage of the wilderness, and now, in the third month after leaving Egypt, they reached Sinai and encamped before the mount.

Here God purposed to give His law for His redeemed people, and to call His faithful servant into nearer and more intimate fellowship with Himself.

We remember that when Moses met God at Mount Horeb, he hid his face in fear; but since then he has been prepared to know

Him more fully by his walk of obedience, and by his entire dependence upon Him. He has gone on "from strength to strength"; and we have seen the shrinking, diffident man transformed into the bold, fearless, faithful servant of the invisible God with whom he had been communing day by day. Thus it is that faith and obedience up to present knowledge of the will of God prepares us for the fuller fellowship we long to know.

After the day when God appeared to Moses as a flame of fire in a bush, we have no record of any further revelation of Himself to him personally until Sinai is reached. All through the conflict with Pharaoh and with the murmuring Israelites on the journey to Sinai, the intercourse between God and His servant is expressed by "the LORD spake to Moses."

But when Mount Sinai is reached, we read that "Moses went up unto God, and the LORD called unto him out of the mountain" (Exodus 19:3). Moses probably sought the Lord, manifested in the pillar of cloud, for the purpose of knowing His mind about the people now assembled at Sinai. And from this point we may see the faithful servant led step by step into nearer and closer fellowship with God, until he was admitted to the glory and the devouring fire at the summit of the mountain . . . coming forth again to walk among men with the light of heaven upon his face, and to be known as the meekest man on the earth.

When the Lord called to him first at Sinai, it was to send him back to Israel with a brief message, embodying the primary conditions upon which God would deal with them as His people.

Moses returns to the Lord with Israel's answer: "All that the LORD hath spoken we will do"; and then he is instructed to prepare them for the third day, when Jehovah would come down upon Mount Sinai and speak to him in their presence and hearing.

After solemn preparation, on the third day Moses led forth the people to meet with God; and as they stood at the foot of the mountain the Lord descended in fire, and the whole mount quaked greatly. When the blast of the trumpet grew louder and louder, Moses spoke, and God answered him by a voice, calling him to the top of the mount.

On the way up he was sent back again, to charge Israel solemnly not to break through and gaze, and perish. Once more he ascends the mountain until he reaches the thick darkness upon the summit. So terrible was the sight that Moses said, "I exceedingly fear and quake" (Hebrews 12:21).

Could this be the same God who had so tenderly and graciously listened to Moses' fears at Horeb? How could he have talked with God so freely?

Very mercifully does the Lord veil Himself to us in early days, and lead us on as we are able to endure, until we can bear some knowledge of His holiness and learn with godly fear and awe that we have to do with One who is consuming fire.

Many of us may have been to Horeb, where we have met the Lord, and where He has been revealed to us as a flame of fire dwelling in us, as He did in that lowly thornbush. We have walked with Him, in obedience and faith, while going forth with the message of deliverance to souls in bondage. We have learned to trust Him in hours of danger. We have sung the song of victory, and, in the testing that followed, have proved the power of the "tree" to change the bitter waters of our own life into the sweet water of the life from heaven.

We have learned the power of uplifted hands to God in the conflict with Amalek, and have faithfully worked with God as He has led us from grace to grace; but how we have longed to know that "face-to-face" fellowship with Him on the mount and hungered for His call, "Come with Me, and look from the top"!

There comes a time with us, as with Moses, when He is revealed to us in the awful majesty of Sinai. Not that we may tremble, as Israel trembled then, but that we may know Him in His righteousness, and have some conception of the exceeding sinfulness of sin, and the holiness of the God who has redeemed us.

The commandments of Jehovah were not made known to Israel when in Egypt. They were brought out without any knowledge of the One who was redeeming them. They came out of Egypt with all their Egyptian habits, and with loose ideas of right and wrong. Not until they were out of bondage, and separated from the old life in Egypt, did God begin to reveal to them something of Himself and the righteousness of life demanded from those who bore His name. It was as much a revelation to Moses as to the people.

The people trembled and stood afar off, but "Moses drew near unto the thick darkness where God was" (Exodus 20:21). It is written that *we* have not come to Mount Sinai, to "blackness and darkness and tempest," but to *Mount Zion*, and to *Jesus the Mediator*, and the blood of sprinkling (Hebrews 12:18–24). At every stage of our spiritual life we have boldness to enter into the Holiest by His blood, and may draw near in full assurance of faith, having our hearts sprinkled from an evil conscience; but before we learn in actual experience to know God "face to face" we may find Him drawing near to us in thick darkness. Not a darkness such as fell upon the Egyptians, but a darkness out of which He speaks and judges our lives, as the Righteous One, until their every detail has been adjusted and brought into accord with His mind.

Moses returns to Israel with the ordinances of God, and after the covenant is entered into and the people have been sprinkled with the blood, Aaron with his two sons, and seventy representatives of Israel, are allowed to go up with Moses to some part of the mount to see the God of Israel. "There was under His feet as it were a work of bright sapphire [like] the very heaven for clearness. . . . And they beheld God, and did eat and drink" (Exodus 24:10–11, *ASV*, margin). The "clearness" is in sharp contrast to the darkness out of which He had given His law to Moses the day before. May not this contrast suggest the effect of the shed blood, which Moses had sprinkled on the people and the book of the covenant at the foot of the mountain before the elders ascended? It is at least true in the gospel of grace. God must judge His children's lives, and in His dealings may lead them through much darkness—but through the blood of Jesus, applied by the Holy Spirit, the darkness passes away, and they emerge into the clear light of heaven with nothing between.

We are told that the elders of Israel saw God "afar off." This vision of God is not the "face-to-face" fellowship that Moses is to know. To "walk in the light as [God] is in the light" (1 John 1:7) is blessed indeed, but we may be drawn nearer still, even *into* Him who is the Light itself—just as from this group, thus privileged to see God, Moses is called forth to *personal* knowledge of the Holy One. "Come up *to Me* into the mount, and *be there*," said Jehovah (Exodus 24:12).

Moses at once obeys the call. Alone he enters the cloud upon the summit, not thick darkness now, but glory, for "the glory of the LORD abode upon Mount Sinai." To the onlookers it was "devouring fire," and Moses was either near or in this devouring fire for forty days and forty nights.

Six days he waited in silence for God to speak. Then God revealed to him the pattern of the tabernacle in which He would dwell in the midst of His people.

How wondrously true to experience the story is! It is in the darkness with God that we learn His judgments; it is in the glory "within the veil" that we are shown His pattern for our lives. It is after the darkness, and the judgments, and the sprinkled blood that we go even part of the way up the mount and have that vision of God where His light streams into our lives and we eat and drink as in His presence, having fellowship one with another, with the blood of Jesus cleansing from all sin; but *alone* we are called to enter the cloud and dwell in the devouring fire—alone, and only alone, we enter the secret place of the Most High, and know Him "face to face."

Six days of silence. Then on the seventh day God spoke to His waiting servant. This reminds us of the six days of creation, when God said, "Let there be," and it was so, and on the seventh day He rested from His work.

Even so the cloud covered the mountain and Moses for the six days, and God waited until His servant was brought into accord with that "sound of gentle stillness" in which God reveals Himself and His will. Here, in the silence, all memory of the camp and its busy life would pass away; all the activity of the creature in mind and thought would be at rest; all burden concerning the need of Israel and the claims of friends would be forgotten.

On the seventh day, the number typifying completion, God was satisfied; His channel of revelation to the people was ready. The pattern shown to Moses in the mount would be given them as he received it, for his mind had been cleared and stilled and emptied of all other things. So it proved: he did nothing but receive; then he was sent back to the camp to give out to others the pattern which he was "caused to see in the mount."

Even so does God need channels today. Souls who will seek to know Him as Moses did, and be willing to be emptied of all their own thoughts and to be drawn aside with Him, drawn even from the very duties committed to them by Him, that they may come forth with the pattern for the building of His spiritual temple and say with God-given assurance, "Thus saith the LORD."

CHAPTER 8

"FACE TO FACE"

"And it came to pass, as Moses entered into the tabernacle, . . . the cloudy pillar descended . . . and the LORD talked with Moses . . . face to face, as a man speaketh unto his friend" (Exodus 33:9, 11).

WHILE Moses was up on the mount, there occurred in the camp the events that drew forth from him the most supreme surrender of his life. Whether one had anything to do with the other we cannot say, but it is after this great crisis we read that "the LORD spake unto Moses face to face, as a man speaketh unto his friend."

When the people saw that Moses, the man upon whom they had relied for communication with God, did not return, they gathered around Aaron and cried, "Up, make us gods, which shall go before us; for as for this Moses, the man that brought us up out of the land of Egypt, we know not what is become of him" (Exodus 32:1, ASV). Their Egyptian life was still strong upon them. The Egyptians had exterior symbols of the gods they worshiped; so must they. Aaron, frightened and weak, yields to the cry of the people, gives them the visible substitute for God they asked for . . . and under the name of worshiping Jehovah, back to Egypt in heart and act the erring people went.

On the mount, God tells Moses what is taking place in the camp, and says, "Let Me alone, . . . that I may consume them; and I will make of thee a great nation" (Exodus 32:10). But Moses knew his God; he had seen what faith could do; and his confidence was in the great compassionate heart of Him who had wrought such mighty deeds for them. In the boldness of faith he holds God to His word, saying, "Remember . . . Thou swarest," and he had power with God and prevailed.

Jehovah had said, "I will make of *thee* a great nation"; but glory at the cost of Israel, Moses did not want. His aim was to bring the people into the promised land. He had so pleaded and suffered for them that his whole heart was filled with intense desire that they should obtain their inheritance.

It is impossible to pray for others and not be consumed with a deep longing to be poured out on their behalf.

Moses could not admit for one moment a thought of glory for himself or his family, and let these souls, so difficultly won and so sorely kept in the path to Canaan, suffer loss. Moses "besought the face of the LORD" (Exodus 32:11, *margin*), and held Him to His word, with the result that "the LORD repented of the evil," and Moses turned and left the Presence, knowing there was now but one thing to do, and that quickly, before the judgment of God broke forth upon their sin.

Out of the stillness of the Holy Presence on the mount, down to the camp he went; and with righteous anger against sin, he took the golden calf, burned it, and ground it to powder. Aaron begs for Moses' understanding, and says, "The people . . . are set on mischief." Whatever the people are set on, it matters not to Moses; he had come from the presence of the Holy God, and the sin and shame of Israel in turning from the Living God to heathen symbols is too vividly before his eyes for him to listen to excuses.

What a night that must have been to Moses as he pondered over the events of the day—pondered and prayed until the passion of longing over the sinning people leads him to a stupendous decision. He cannot bear to think that, after all the travail, Israel might lose the inheritance and forfeit the presence of their God.

When morning dawns he says to the people, "Ye have sinned a great sin: and now I will go up unto the LORD; peradventure I shall make an atonement for your sin" (Exodus 32:30). Back to the mount he goes. Step by step he climbs, never swerving in his purpose, until he reaches the Presence and makes his bold request, "If Thou wilt, forgive. . . . If not, blot me, I pray Thee, out of Thy book" (Exodus 32:32).

In effect he offers to sacrifice, for the sake of Israel, every reward for which he had surrendered the pleasures and treasures of Egypt when he made his choice in the court of Pharaoh. He had then chosen the path of the cross with a hope of ultimate gain, but in close fellowship with God he had so entered the divine attitude of sacrifice that all self-seeking has passed away.

It has been said that *fellowship* is more than partnership: it is a blending of spirit with spirit, of heart with heart, so that no words are needed, for the two are one.

It is only possible to understand the words of Moses by knowing, and sharing, the attitude of Christ that lies behind them, for they speak of an intensity of self-surrender that few of us have known. Those who have entered into the afflictions of Christ for His Church's sake know something of what they mean, for they have learned in a measure to pour out their souls unto death, in fellowship with Him—not as sharing in His atonement, but in fulfillment of the law of sacrifice for life to flow to others.

Speaking reverently, and knowing the heart of God as we have seen it revealed in the Lord Jesus Christ, Jehovah must have been deeply moved as He looked at His pleading servant, for back in the ages of eternity the Lamb, slain from the foundation of the world, had offered Himself to His Father as an atonement for the sins of the people.

Jehovah had been showing Moses His plan for teaching Israel the meaning of sacrifice for sin. He had told him of the types which would foreshadow to the world the Son of God who was to be offered up at the place called Calvary as the fulfiller of all the types, even as the one perfect and sufficient sacrifice for the sins of the whole world.

As Moses listened to God's directions about the brazen altar, and the great need of atonement, when Israel's sin would be put away by the blood of bulls and of goats, he understood, as never before, why they had been sheltered from the destroyer in Egypt by the blood of a slain lamb. He saw *sin from the standpoint of God,* and the need of atonement, and so deeply did this revelation enter into his soul that, as he pondered over the great sin of Israel, the thought entered his mind that God *might* accept *him* as an atonement and pardon the people.

At all events, he resolved to identify himself with Israel and suffer with them. How little Moses knew that he was typifying the only-begotten Son of God who, manifest in human form, identified Himself with sinners, and "Him who knew no sin [was] made to be sin on our behalf, that we might become the righteousness of God in Him" (2 Corinthians 5:21, *ASV*).

The divine Spirit had so permeated this man of God that now he looks at Israel from *His* standpoint, and is moved with unspeakable pity for them. In truth, the world can never be the same to him again, for he has been drawn into union with the very heart of God, and must of necessity come forth sharing His attitude of compassion for sinners, while hating their sin.

In reply to the petition of Moses, the Lord simply bids him go and lead the people into the land. His offer could not be accepted, but he was heard, in that the nation was not cast off—though the inevitable consequence of their sin would follow.

From this time Moses was granted a closer fellowship with Jehovah than before. He had hitherto gone up to the mount when called, but now he has free access to the immediate presence of God, in a "Tent of Meeting" set apart for the purpose and pitched outside the camp (Exodus 33:7, ASV). When he went out to the Tent, the wondrous sight was seen of the cloudy pillar descending and standing at the door, while inside "the LORD talked with Moses," and spoke to him "face to face, as a man speaketh unto his friend." "With him will I speak mouth to mouth, even manifestly, and not in dark speeches" (Numbers 12:8, ASV).

We are given a glimpse into one interview at this time between God and His "friend," a glimpse unveiling to us the inner life of Moses as it progressed ever more and more into oneness with God.

In all the previous interviews we have seen him in the Presence on behalf of the people: at Horeb, to receive his commission; then at Sinai, first to learn the various laws, and afterwards, in the forty days at the summit, to be shown the pattern of the Tabernacle, where God would dwell in the midst of Israel.

But the veil is lifted to show us the friendship to which he has been admitted since that great surrender for the sake of the people. The one desire of Moses is now, "Show me now Thy way, that I may *know Thee*" (Exodus 33:13). He has passed beyond all things to God Himself, and when the promise is given, "My face shall go with thee" (verse 14, *lit.*), Moses grows bolder, and says, "I beseech Thee, show me Thy glory." Through the words of the Lord Jesus we understand what he asked; for the Son of God, when on earth, unfolded the purposes of God as they had been in His heart from all eternity, and said of His redeemed ones, "The glory which Thou gavest Me I have given them; that they may be one, even as We are one. . . . Father, I will that they also, whom Thou hast given Me, be with Me where I am, that they may behold My glory" (John 17:22–24).

Jehovah replies to Moses, "There shall no man see Me and live," and then fore-shadows His plan whereby His banished may be restored to Him. As accursed ones they cannot see Him and live, but, hidden in the cleft Rock—the wounded side of Him who in the fullness of time would die for them that they might die in Him, and *in Him* pass into the place prepared for them— they will behold the glory of God in the face of Jesus Christ, who is the outshining of His glory and the express image of His Person.

After the interview in the "Tent of Meeting," Moses is bidden to present himself once more at the summit of the mount, and the Lord descended and stood with him there, and proclaimed His name, giving him such a revelation of His character and grace that Moses made haste and bowed himself to the earth and worshiped.

Forty days and forty nights did Moses spend again on the mount, and later on he tells Israel what occurred during this second prolonged communion with God. "I fell down before the LORD . . . forty days and forty nights . . . because of all your sins. . . . I prayed for Aaron also the same time" (Deuteronomy 9:18–20).

Forty days of intercession for the people followed his stupendous offer to suffer on their behalf; and when he returns to the camp his face shines with reflected glory, though he realized it not. So unearthly was this glory that Aaron and the people were afraid to come near him, until he called out and talked to them as of old; but, so little can those who know not the Lord fully bear even the reflection of His light, Moses found it necessary to put a veil over his face while he talked with them. Truly it was the Presence that separated between him and his fellows, and his difficulty now was to get others to be at ease with him, for he was the "man Moses" after all!

He was veiled to men but unveiled to God, for the veil was taken away when he went in to speak to the Lord, and replaced when he came out to move among men. What loneliness, what isolation this meant to him, for he could not have close fellowship with Jehovah without separation from others. This is what "face-to-face" fellowship with God means. On the Godward side, a life "with unveiled face beholding as in a mirror the glory of the Lord," and "transformed into the same image from glory to glory" (2 Corinthians 3:18, *ASV*), yet, by the unconscious, unavoidable effect of that intimacy with God, veiled to others and separated from the things of earth, as one "not living in the world"; veiled also under the covering of the most ordinary life, "as unknown, and yet well known; as dying, and behold, we live; as chastened, and not killed"; "pressed on every side, yet not straitened; perplexed, yet not unto despair; . . . always delivered unto death for Jesus' sake, that the life also of Jesus may be manifested in our mortal flesh. For we have this treasure in earthen vessels, that the exceeding greatness of the power may be of God, and not from ourselves" (2 Corinthians 6:9; 4:7–11, *ASV*).

It has been pointed out that from this time forth the chief work of Moses was to communicate the will of God to the people, and it is written that he was "very meek, above all the men which were upon the face of the earth" (Numbers 12:3). This is the mark of the heavenly life, and the result of intimate relationship with God. Jesus, the Holy Son of God, said of Himself, "I am meek and lowly in heart"; and just in proportion as we share His life, and are conformed to His image, shall we manifest the meek and quiet spirit so precious in the sight of God.

The meekness of this man who saw God "face to face" shines out again and again in his later life. His sorrows and outward trials grew more and more severe through the very souls that had already cost him so much, and he was tested on every hand. He had to learn fellowship with the long-suffering God, and bear and suffer with the people to the end.

In trial after trial the heavenly spirit shone forth. Moses' freedom from all self-glory was evidenced in his response to Joshua—jealous for his leader—when he said, "Enviest thou for my sake? Would God that all the LORD'S people were prophets" (Numbers 11:29). And his silence when Miriam and Aaron spoke against him (Numbers 12) also shows the spirit of the Lamb.

But the veil is drawn over his sufferings when, after all that he had gone through on their behalf, the event he dreaded came about and Israel was turned back into the wilderness when on the very edge of the promised land. Even while Moses was with them, some of the people actually proposed to elect a captain to take them back to Egypt, and once more God threatened to smite them and offered to make Moses the founder of a chosen people. Had he accepted the offer he would not have needed to spend the weary years that followed in bearing with the wayward nation. But again he turns from all thought of self-interest and deliberately chooses to share their lot.

For nearly forty years they wandered in the wilderness, their much-tried leader with them, until at the close it even went ill with him for their sakes. Wearied with that great and terrible wilderness, and with the ceaseless murmurings and unbelief of the people, he "spoke unadvisedly with his lips." God had said "Speak to the rock," but in the bitterness of his soul Moses forgot to walk softly with his God. He *struck* the rock twice and thus failed to obey God implicitly. God could not overlook a single lapse into disobedience in the one who stood for righteousness before the people. Sin must be judged, whether in Moses or Israel. The greater his privilege of knowing God "face to face," the greater the sin of the least unfaithfulness—and so the word passed, "Because ye trespassed, . . . because ye sanctified Me not in the midst of the children of Israel, . . . thou shalt see the land before thee; but thou shalt not go thither" (Deuteronomy 32:51–52).

"Behold, therefore, the goodness and severity of God: on [him] . . . severity; but toward thee, goodness, if thou continue in His goodness; otherwise—" (Romans

11:22). Let us be not high-minded, but fear.

Once more Moses ascends a mountain, the mount of Pisgah—and there he beholds the land of promise. There he died, and was buried by God Himself. One hundred and twenty years old, his eye not dim, and his natural force not abated, unworn and uncrushed notwithstanding all the sorrow and suffering of those years in the wilderness—for his God had been his strength.

UNION WITH CHRIST
IN DEATH AND RESURRECTION

*Three Conference Addresses
in Summarized Form*

INTRODUCTION

MY theme for this conference is "The Deeper Aspect of the Death of Christ, in Its Bearing upon the Present Hour." It does intensely bear upon the present hour, for unless we get down to the bedrock meaning of the cross in actual, living experience, we shall be unable to stand against the pressure of the world, the flesh, and the devil in the present state of things in the world.

Let me say at the outset that it may appear in the first part of my message that I am going again over ground familiar to you, but this is necessary for the sake of many who have not been in our conferences before.

There are three main aspects of the death of Christ which it is important clearly to recognize as being distinct the one from the other. (1) The first is the *objective fact* of our identification with Christ in His death, so that we are said to have utterly and entirely died in Him as our substitute. We find this set forth in Romans 6:1–6. (2) The second is the *subjective,* or experiential, outworking of the first—the "making to die" the "doings of the body," which means the application of the death of Christ to the believer "through the Spirit" (Romans 8:13). (3) Then we have the third aspect which follows when the life of Christ imparted to us on the basis of our death-union with Him is brought into full maturity. This we find referred to in Philippians 3:10 where, in *"the power of His resurrection,"* we enter into "the fellowship of His sufferings" for the Church, and are made "conformable to His death." "For those whom He foreknew, He also predestined to be made like to the pattern of His Son, that many brethren might be joined to Him, the firstborn" (Romans 8:29, *CH*). "Like in *suffering*" is the footnote to Conybeare's rendering, with a reference to Philippians 3:10.

CHAPTER 1

THE DEATH-IDENTIFICATION
MESSAGE

LET us turn to Romans 6 for the basic
fact of our identification with Christ in
His death. Note the words *"His death."*
"How shall we that are *dead*" (verse 2);
"baptized into *His death*" (verse 3); "he that
is *dead*" (verse 7); "if we be *dead*" (verse 8).
The Lexicon says that here the word "to
die," in the Greek, has a prefix rendering
the verb vivid and intense, *representing an
action that is consummated and finished.*
The same word is used in 2 Corinthians
5:14, "If one died for all, then were all
dead." Again in Colossians 2:20, "If ye be
dead with Christ," and Colossians 3:3, "For
ye are *dead. . . .*"

Let us face again what this means.
Clearly it says that the believer is so identi-
fied with Christ in His death that when
Christ died, in the eye of God *he* died. In

brief, "when Jesus went to Calvary, He took the *sinner* too!" The language of the Greek original is quite plain, and in every passage repeated—"If we be *dead*," "for ye are *dead*"—at least six times over.*

This makes the *objective* fact of our identification with Christ in His death quite clear. There is no "process of death" referred to in these passages. Nothing of the "subjective." That comes in elsewhere. My concern now is to stress the objective fact which is plainly stated as the substitutionary meaning of the cross, where we understand that Christ was made sin for us and bore our sins in His own body on the tree.

But you say, "I have known and seen this for years, but it does not appear to make any difference in my life." Here comes in the need of recognizing the Holy Spirit, who is the Spirit of revelation. There are a large number of God's children in these recent years who have been accepting the "truth" of death with Christ, but it has not come to them in the power of the Holy Spirit. They say that they are "crucified with Christ," but they know that for some reason they cannot fathom, the acceptance of this truth has not made the difference to them in practical life which they had ex-

---

*Romans 6:2, 7, 8; 2 Corinthians 5:14; Colossians 2:20; Colossians 3:3; 2 Timothy 2:11.

pected. One reason is that, in some cases, the truth has been received only by the mind, apart from that deep surrender to God which is necessary for the working of the Holy Spirit in the life, as well as for His unveiling of the "eyes of the heart" (Ephesians 1:18, *CH*) of the believer concerning all that the death and resurrection of Christ meant in the purposes of God.

Another reason why many have not realized the power of the truth is that they confuse the objective fact of their death with Christ with the *subjective outworking of it.* The Scripture tells you to "work out your own salvation," but those of you who are properly instructed know that we "work out our own salvation" only after we have received it through the blood of Christ. Exactly in the same way we must first apprehend, through the revelation of the Holy Spirit, that we died together with Christ when He hung on the cross, and on the basis of that fact proceed to "work it out." Not understanding this subjective "working out," many ignore the objective fact they have really apprehended, saying "it doesn't work."

THE MOMENT OF IDENTIFICATION

But now there is an important point here which Philip Mauro makes clear in one of his books. The question arises as to *when* "identification" of the believer with Christ in His death actually began. Mauro says that it began *"at the moment of Christ's death, and not before."* The believer is not in any way associated with the sufferings of Christ in His propitiatory work as the Lamb of God bearing away the sin of the world. It was after He had cried with a loud voice, "It is finished," that the God-Man "dismissed His spirit" (Luke 23:46; Matthew 27:50, *Scofield*) and died. It was at the moment of His *death* that believers were identified with Him in that death, and died with Him. Mauro points out that in Romans 6:10, where it is written "In that HE DIED, . . ." the verb signifies the exit from the body.

All the language used about our identification with Christ in death is clear. We are "baptized into His *death.*" It is hardly necessary to say that this does not mean into His actual *physical* death at Golgotha with all the anguish and horror and darkness of His cross, which preceded the moment of His death. He accomplished the work of redemption alone. He could say "It is finished," so that when He reached the actuality of death all for whom He died died with Him, and united to Him passed with Him into another sphere—alive unto God "IN CHRIST JESUS."

THE LIFE-POWER
OF THE IDENTIFICATION

"Reckon ye also yourselves to be dead indeed unto sin, but ALIVE unto God through Jesus Christ" (Romans 6:11). The identification-union with Christ in His death is most truly an "attitude," and a "position" to be maintained in reliance upon the Spirit of God in His enabling power; but it is also to be made a fact in the believer's *experience,* just as much as his deliverance from the burden of sin. The failure to see this explains the absence of life-power even when maintaining the position and attitude of "death with Christ." We need to see that a real identification-union with Christ in His death, *brought about by the Holy Spirit* by His co-working with the believer's apprehension of the truth, has LIFE in it as well as "death."

We think of the word "death" in human values, but Dr. Mabie writes that "Christ's death was not an ordinary death," but "an entirely new and original kind of death." "So far from being mere mortal dying," it might "rather be called *immortal* dying." "It contains," he says, "within itself the ENERGY OF A NEW ORGANIC UNION WITH THE RISEN CHRIST HIMSELF." He says, "This death was such a death that when, in its whole fact and energy, it comes to exercise itself, it *provides the dynamic* needed to enter into the believer and empower him to live the new life to which the death of Christ has committed him."*

Elsewhere, Dr. Mabie again writes that the death of Christ is "radioactive." I asked a medical man the other day to tell me something about radium, and he said, "Radium is the strongest concentrated force that the world knows, and it has the power of contributing its energy or power to everything in its vicinity." "Yes," said a missionary. "If you come under its direct rays you may be killed, for it burns you."

May this not be the reason why there is no *life* realized as the result of apprehending the death-identification aspect of the cross? What Mabie calls "mere mortal dying" has no "life" in it, nor does it contain "radioactive" power. We have talked of resurrection "life" but failed to get it in the abundant measure we desire because we have not seen *that that life is the death* of the God-Man, and will be *communicated to us in dynamic power only as we actually*

---

*Dr. Mabie's books, from which these sentences are taken, are entitled: *The Meaning and Message of the Cross; The Divine Reason of the Cross.* Published by Fleming H. Revell, New York. A third volume, published by Hodder & Stoughton, London, is entitled, *How Does the Death of Christ Save Us?* We fear all are now out of print, but they are of the highest value.

*and continuously come under the power of
that divine death* in its mighty working.

There are some more quotations from Dr.
Mabie which I must give you before I pass
on. Writing of the necessity for the subjective as well as the objective teaching of the
cross, he says: "Leave out the substitutionary objective, and you have lost the chief
potency for securing the subjective experience. Omit the subjective—the very point
in experience where the substitutionary
work passes into personal, transforming
power—and you have *vitiated the composite death-resurrection energy of Christ
mid-process. . . .*" Here it is clear: if you
omit the "substitutionary *objective,*" then
you do not get the "subjective." Omit the
subjective (and that is what most people
do), and you *"vitiate the composite death-
resurrection energy"* of Christ to save us.
You must have the two sides, the *objective*
work of Christ for your faith, and the *subjective* application of it to be wrought into
experience by the Holy Spirit.

"The objective and subjective are correla-
tive to each other as substance and
shadow," again writes Dr. Mabie; "they each
imply the other," and there is "a new vital
energy working in the soul, making the
whole process profoundly *ethical.*"

THE REALITY OF
THE IDENTIFICATION-UNION

We have seen clearly that we can only apprehend our union with Christ in His death at Calvary by the revelation and co-working operation of the Holy Spirit. Now let us see how He works in co-operating power. Verse 5 of Romans 6 gives this in a few brief words. "If we have been *planted together* in the likeness of His death." This means something more than the "likeness" of passing beneath water and out in a few brief moments. To be "planted" into the "likeness of His death" carries in the words a mystical union brought about by the Spirit of God. J. N. Darby's footnote to this verse says that "planted" is not the clearest expression of the meaning of the original. He says, "It means literally 'grown up with' and so 'thoroughly one' . . ." The believer, by some operation of the Spirit, is to become "thoroughly one" with the death of Christ, so that, as it were, "planted" into it, he "grows up" in its pattern or likeness.

The fact of verse 2, "we that are *dead*," is opened out into fuller explanation of its meaning in verse 5. The purpose of God is manifestly that the believer is to be so conformed to the death of Christ that the life of Christ in him will grow up into the pattern of the Lambhood nature of Christ. Like the grain of wheat which falls into the ground to die to bring forth much fruit, the believer is in some mystical way to be united with the First Grain of wheat in such a way that through him also life will produce fruit (John 12:24).

Conybeare's rendering of verse 5 is even more striking. It runs, "If we have been *grafted* into the likeness of His death." The footnote adds, "Literally, have become partakers of a *vital union*, as that of a graft with the tree into which it is grafted."

Such a "grafting" can only be done by the Holy Spirit. In both cases—the "growing up together" so as to become "thoroughly one," and the being "grafted" into His death— there is the same objective. The identification-union with Christ in His death must be made a fact in experience as well as a fact to be apprehended by faith in the Word of God.*

This is the sum of the whole matter at this stage: from the moment you are "planted" into the death of Christ, so that

---

*A striking metaphor used by the Apostle in Romans 6:17 confirms this aspect of the death fellowship with Christ. He says that we are to obey from the heart "the teaching" whereby we are "molded anew" (CH)—a metaphor from the casting of metals. The "death of Christ is likened to a mold" (Dr. Marsh), into which the believer is cast for molding into its likeness.

you grow up into Christ in His likeness, *for the rest of your life "His death" lies at the root of your entire Christian life.* "If we have been grafted. . . ." A graft is put into a tree to become one with the tree, with the intention that there shall be ONE LIFE flowing through both. Have you fully apprehended the fact of your identification with Christ at the moment that He died, so that you have become a partaker of a vital union as that of a graft with the tree into which it is grafted?

CHAPTER 2

THE DEATH-IDENTIFICATION APPLIED

N OW WE TURN to the second, or subjective, aspect of the death of Christ in
its practical application to the "flesh" or
Adamic life of nature in the redeemed believer. Read Romans 7:4–5.

"Ye are also *become dead* . . . by the
body of Christ. . . . For when we were in
the flesh, the motions of sins . . . did work
in our members. . . ."

The Greek word "dead" in this passage is
different from all the others quoted in Romans 6:2, 7, 8; Colossians 3:3, etc. It is
"*thanatoo*," not "*apothenesko*." The Lexicon
says that "*thanatoo*" means "to take away
the vital principle," "to cause to be put to
death." It is the word used in Romans 8:13,
"through the Spirit 'mortify,' or *make to die*
[margin] the deeds of the body." Here we
have very clearly the subjective outworking, or application in detail to the life of the

flesh, of the identification fact which the believer has already apprehended, and had made real to him in the power of the Spirit. *"Planted into the likeness of His death,"* "grafted" into his place in identification-union with Christ, so that the dynamic force of His death has full power of action, the believer has now to have this applied to the *"doings of the body"*—the possible "motions of sins" in his "members"—which have perpetually to be reckoned with as requiring the keen watchful "making to die," if the *identification-union with Christ* is to progress into a life of full conformity to Christ.

To realize the need of this continuous application of Christ's death in "making to die" the deeds of the body, we must first get a clear sight of what the Scriptures teach about "flesh" and "spirit," and the way in which the "flesh" has to be dealt with so that the Spirit may rule, for unless we are able to recognize the "flesh" when it seeks to break in, and know how to deal with it at once, the power of the central identification will be nullified. For it must be emphasized that, however deeply we may be "planted" into the death of Christ in the innermost part of our being, there always will exist the necessity of watchfulness against the "motions of sin" in our members breaking out into action in some degree.

But first as to what Paul says about the

"flesh." By it he means the *entire Adamic nature* with which we are born (John 3:6; Ephesians 2:3; Colossians 2:13). Even as Jesus declared (John 6:63), the flesh—human strength—counts for nothing, so far as producing spiritual life. What the "flesh" is Godward we see in Romans 8:7–8. It is in its essence "enmity against God," and "cannot please God." What the "flesh" is manward we find summarized in Galatians 5:19–21: "The works of the flesh are manifest. . . ." In these few verses you have grouped a vivid picture of the various phases of its workings: (1) in gross physical sins; (2) in evil dispositions, of hatred, strife, jealousy, bad temper, dissension and selfish ambition; (3) in religious forms of intrigues, divisions, sectarian parties; (4) in evil supernatural fellowship with Satan in idolatry and witchcraft; (5) in self-indulgence, in drunkenness and revelings. All these "works" are easily recognized, and most believers imagine they are wholly free from "walking after the flesh" because they think only of "flesh" as meaning the various phases of its characteristics as given here. They do not realize that the "flesh" means "flesh" even when it works in a more refined form. What about strife, jealousy, bad temper, selfish ambition and *sectarian parties*, as included in the list with the more fleshly sins? And they do not realize that they can "walk after the flesh" at any moment unless they are walking after the Spirit, "making to die" the "deeds of the body" so as to be truly led by the Spirit as sons of God.

To see this clearly we must go back again to Romans 7:5. "When we were in the flesh," said Paul, "the motions of sin did work in our members." And *they always will work at any stage of the believer's life,* as soon as he ceases to "walk after the Spirit" with the Adamic nature under the radioactive power of Christ's death.

The whole of the seventh of Romans after verse 5 is an inspired picture of the actual condition of the believer as he is in himself, and as he *will always be in himself* should he cease to walk in the Spirit at any moment. Some think that Romans seven lies between chapter six and chapter eight as a sort of passage between, and that when the believer emerges into Romans eight, Romans seven becomes past history; but Dr. Andrew Murray says that Romans seven and Romans eight may be described as being *simultaneous states,* either of which the believer walks after according to his choice.[*] This appears to be correct, from Paul's concluding words in verse 25, "So THEN, with the *mind* I myself serve the law of God, but

---

[*]See pp. 117–118, *"The Spirit of Christ."*

with the flesh the law of sin." That is, *the "flesh" is the flesh, all the way along,* and although we may not and need not "walk" or "live" "after the flesh," the "deeds of the body" will always have to be "made to die" if we are always to be "led of the Spirit" and be kept free from coming under the power of the law of sin and death.

The apprehension of this solemn fact is of the most vital importance at the present hour, for among many who are pressing on into the knowledge of the life in the heavenlies there is the danger of assuming they are beyond the possibility of the inroads of the "flesh," especially if they are seeking to know the life of Jesus manifested in their mortal bodies. They speak of being "new creations in Christ"—and they are, but we have not yet *"new creation"* bodies. Our present bodies of humiliation await the advent of the Lord from heaven before they are conformed to the body of His glory. A *grave danger at the present moment is the premature appropriation of truth*—a stretching beyond "that which is written" (1 Corinthians 4:6), for if the devil cannot get a believer down into the manifest "flesh," he just gives him a push into a spirit-sphere where he gets out of focus with the central base of the cross and into a hyper-spirituality which eventually means a spiritualized "flesh." "Error," it has been said, is just "truth" pushed a shade too far, and thus thrown out of perspective with other truth that makes up a balanced and symmetrical whole. We may also be sure that under cover of this the "flesh" will begin to work in some insidious form unheeded and unrecognized.

Now as to the practical application of the death of Christ, and how it has to be done. Again let us turn to Romans 8:13 in conjunction with Romans 7:4, because in these two passages the same Greek word is used. We have seen clearly that when the identification fact is definitely appropriated there is always the practical dealing with the "body" and its "members" to follow.

In Romans 8:13 we are told that we have to mortify or "make to die" the "deeds of the body," but it is *"by the Spirit."* What does this mean? Just this: the believer "makes to die" the "doings" of his body by reliance upon the Holy Spirit as he appropriates his death with Christ. "Ye are *become dead* . . ." writes Paul. He already is "dead" by identification-union; he now *reckons* that he is "dead" to the "motions of sins in his members" as he finds them arise. "The cross of Christ," wrote the late C. A. Fox, "is the divine laboratory where the flesh is cauterized, and put to death. . . . Mortify your members accordingly, which are upon the earth, by applying instantly the burning caustic of the cross to every tempting appetite before it can rise. . . ."

This language is wondrously like Dr. Mabie's words of the death of Christ being "radioactive." Yes, this is the blessed fact we need to understand: *the "death" of Christ has in it dynamic power.* The entire Adamic nature, described as "flesh"—always ready to break out in the "motions of sins" in our members—must be deprived of its power by the application of the "caustic," or radioactiveness, of that death *which was more than a human death.* Then, blessed be God, as the "caustic" is applied by the Holy Ghost, the life of God inherent in that death will rise in quickening power, enabling the believer to walk in victory. For it was only He who was "God manifest in the flesh" that could go down into death and rise out of it, bringing with Him all those who, in the potential purpose of God, died in Him, and now, baptized into that death, realize in Him a continual experience of newness of life to His glory.

"Give therefore unto death your earthly members," O child of God, and set your heart on things above, "for ye *are dead,* and your life is hid with Christ in God" (Colossians 3:3, 5).

CHAPTER 3

THE DEATH FELLOWSHIP IN EXPERIENCE

THE THIRD ASPECT of the fellowship of the believer with Christ in His death which we must now ponder over is of the deepest moment to our risen and ascended Lord, and to His Body the Church, at the present hour.

The passage which brings out this aspect we are most of us familiar with, and yet every time we turn to it we are conscious we have but touched the fringe of its fathomless depths in relation to the cross. Let us turn to 2 Corinthians 4:10–12, Conybeare's translation: "In my body I bear about continually the dying of Jesus, that in my body the life also of Jesus might be shown forth." Literally it is the "killing of Jesus"—the word rendered "dying" is *nekrosis*, quite a different word to those used in Romans 6 and Romans 8:13. Here the Lexicon says, *"It is expressive of the action as incomplete and in progress."*

Conybeare's footnote says, "The word translated 'dying' here is properly the deadness of a corpse, as though St. Paul would say 'my body is not better than a corpse, yet a corpse which shares the life-giving power of Christ's resurrection.'" *"Always bearing about in the body the dying of Jesus . . .* for we which live are always delivered to death," runs the *KJ* rendering.*

The word "always" is the keyword here, for it shows that the death-fellowship must persistently be recognized and deepened if there is to be a full impartation of resurrection life to the "mortal body" as the "making to die" of the "doings of the body" is steadfastly carried out.

There is no real impartation of "resurrection life" apart from the continuous death-identification with Christ. Here again Mabie's words are illuminating: "You cannot separate death and resurrection. They are twin parts of one fact." "The death of Christ carries resurrection in it." If we have

---

*A correspondent who is a skilled Greek scholar writes in respect to this footnote, "There is no means of passing from the *'thanatoo'* experience of Romans 8:13 to the *'nekrosis'* experience of 2 Corinthians 4:10–12 without having first taken exercise at Colossians 3:5, in the deadening process, without which the believer's body will always refuse to be handled as a 'corpse.'"

apprehended the Romans 6 aspect, and seen the aorist tense of the words, that our death with Christ is a consummated fact; and if we have passed on to see that the yielding to death of our "earthly members" is a continuously necessary line of action if our death-union with Christ is not to be rendered null and void; if at this point we fail to apprehend the impartation of resurrection life, the *"power"* of the "resurrection" will be absent. That is, we shall be living in the power of the natural man disguised as "spiritual," and the true, actual impartation of the very life of Jesus—that life which He now has in the glory—will be absent.

It cannot therefore be over-emphasized at this point that all resurrection life is imparted to us *only as we reckon upon our death-union with Christ.* It comes to us from the risen Lord every moment, *via His death,* and as soon as we are out of focus with His death, that impartation of resurrection-life ceases. The center may abide unshaken, but there is an immediate check in the impartation of life to the *circumference,* and an immediate check to the outflow of life to others. The language may be unchanged, the mind retain its knowledge of truth, the will and faith be unaltered, but—*life from the risen Lord has ceased to flow,* for all that was kept out of its way by the continuous death-union has again intervened, and the "body" which may be "no better than a corpse" has ceased to be quickened by the "life-giving power of Christ's resurrection."

There is a law of God, a natural law, which is analagous to this aspect of our death-union with Christ. We know that in the physical frame there is a death-process and a life-process going on continuously, and that one must not exceed the other for normal health. We must equally recognize the same law in what Mabie calls *"the composite death-resurrection energy"* of the principle of the cross. Swing too far into endeavor to lay hold of all that the "new creation" means for spirit, soul and body, without the *necessary death-fellowship* maintained and deepened, and the believer not only will be holding "truth" which has no power in it, but he becomes open to the deceiving spirits of the air, who are only too ready to give the counterfeit of all the "new creation" aspects of truth the soul has eagerly stretched forward to apprehend.

Is it not clear, therefore, how vital is this aspect of the death-union of the cross! It touches the need of the moment at every point, and shows that the one primary message at this time is the cross in all its aspects. It is the one message which will counter the wiles of Satan in every phase of his working among the children of God at the present time.

Now let us look into the way in which this "bearing about in the body the dying of Jesus" may be brought about, and some other results from it in the believer himself. The verse we have quoted is a climax to a few words giving a glimpse into the circumstantial environment of the apostle at the time he wrote, showing that to the believer who knows his death-identification union with Christ, *all external happenings to him are to be read in the light of his death-union with the Lord.* "Troubled," "perplexed," "persecuted," "cast down"—all goes toward the deepening of his death-fellowship with Christ. He may not be given, like Him, an actual "cross," but he will be given all that went toward that "putting to death of Jesus" at Calvary; and the *believer must read his environing circumstances in that light.* They are directly by God's permission for the purpose of bringing about in deepening measure his conformity to that death.

Then let us note what we may call the *deliberateness* of this objective. The Holy Spirit, who has brought about this fellowship, actually again and again hands over to death the believer who fully purposes to know the very "life of Jesus" made "manifest in his mortal flesh." If he wants all that the "new creation" means, then there is no other way but to be prepared to be "delivered unto death for Jesus' sake" as he is able to bear it.

Two results will accrue of deepest moment to the Church of God and to the believer himself. The first we find in verse 12. *"So then, death worketh in us but life in you."* What a fathomless depth we get a glimpse into here! "Death in us"—*"life in you."* Is not that the very crux of the death of Christ Himself? "Death" to Him, life to us. Jukes has a word here of deep significance. He writes, "May we not also, as Christ's members, become ourselves *sacramental*, like His wounded hands and side, giving forth water and blood."

Is there not a hint of this in verse 11— *"For Jesus' sake"*? Here comes in at last such deep union with the risen Lord that the believer can say, "I fill up what is lacking of the sufferings of Christ in my flesh, on behalf of His Body . . ." (Colossians 1:24, *CH*), and "the sufferings of Christ have come upon me" (2 Corinthians 1:5). This is clearly not the Romans 6 "death" to sin, nor the "making to die" of the "doings of the body" of Romans 8:13. The death-union has now become so deep that, like the Lord Himself, the believer is living in this world only to be reckoned "as sheep for the slaughter." "Killed all the day long" (Romans 8:36), sacramentally being poured out as a drink-offering for life to others (see Philippians 2:17, *CH*).

The other result in this deep death-union with Christ is to the believer himself, in his deepening conformity to the pattern of the Christ, in what Mabie describes as His "Lambhood nature." Let us look at Romans 8:29 for a glimpse into this. It reads, "Those He foreknew He also predestinated to be made like to the pattern of His Son."

"Like in suffering" is Conybeare's footnote. Look now at Hebrews 2:10. "In bringing many sons to glory, to consecrate by *sufferings* the Captain. . . ." Literally, says the Conybeare footnote, "to bring to the appointed accomplishment, to develop the full ideal of the character." The full ideal of the pattern of the Son required "suffering" to bring it into full accomplishment. The believer is to be "made like to the pattern." If "suffering" was necessary for the Son, so also it is necessary for all who are "joined to Him, the First-born." If He "learned obedience by the things which He *suffered*"— even so those who are to be conformed to His image. Here then is the key to Philippians 3:10: "That I may know Him, and the power of His resurrection, and the fellowship of His sufferings, being made *conformable unto His death*." The "conformity" to His death is one aspect of our becoming conformable to His likeness in the body of His glory.

Now, lastly, a word on "Throne life" in

relation to this death-fellowship with Christ. Let us not forget that the Throne in Heaven has in the midst of it "a Lamb as it had been [newly] slain" (Revelation 5:6). You may think of "death with Christ" only in its aspect of Golgotha, but *that death is an ever-living power in the heart of the Throne in Heaven.* Because it was no merely human death, but the death of the Son of God, it has in it an ever-fresh dynamic power in the Throne of Heaven. "Resurrection" was in the death on Golgotha, and the Lamb slain is in the center of that Throne in Heaven.

The true "Throne life" authority in Christ which belongs to all united to Him is only to be actually exercised as the believer is deeply centered in his death-identification union. 1 Corinthians 4 gives a glimpse into this. You can see the spurious and the true in their contrasting characteristics in this passage. Verse 8 describes the "spiritualized flesh" apprehending "Throne life"—"Ye have already eaten to the full of spiritual food. Ye are already rich, ye have seated yourselves upon your throne"—and verses 9–13 depict the true "Throne life" of the one who is truly sharing the "composite death-resurrection energy" of fellowship with the Lord. "We are," said Paul, "like criminals condemned to die, to be gazed at by the whole world, both men and angels. . . .

Curses we meet with blessing, persecution with patience, railings with good words. . . ." Here is manifested the Lambhood nature of Him who is as a Lamb in the midst of the Throne of Heaven.

Particulars of the magazine
"The Overcomer"
may be obtained from:

The Overcomer Literature Trust
9-11 Clothier Road
Brislington, Bristol
Avon, BS4 5RL, England

This book was produced by the Christian Literature Crusade. We hope it has been helpful to you in living the Christian life. CLC is a literature mission with ministry in over 45 countries worldwide. If you would like to know more about us, or are interested in opportunities to serve with a faith mission, we invite you to write to:

Christian Literature Crusade
P.O. Box 1449
Fort Washington, PA 19034